CAN YOU FIND MY LOVE?™

BABIES

JAN MARQUART

www.CanYouFindMyLove.com

ISBN: 099733083X
ISBN-13: 9780997330830

Cover and Interior by Publish Pros
www.publishpros.com

Books currently available in the "Can You Find My Love?" Series

Other Books by Jan Marquart

FOR ADULTS

Write to Heal

The Mindful Writer, Still the Mind, Free the Pen

The Basket Weaver, a Novel

Kate's Way, a Novel

Echoes from the Womb, a Book for Daughters

Voices from the Land

The Breath of Dawn, a Journey of Everyday Blessings

How to Write From Your Heart (booklet)

How to Write Your Own Memoir (booklet)

A Manual on How to Deal With a Bully in the Workplace

Cracked Open, a Book of Poems

A Writer's Wisdom

To:

_____

NAME

To Rich Carnahan of Publish Pros, thank you for working so diligently on this book. Your creative energy in design and editing, and your personal touch in producing another book in the Can You Find My Love? children's book series, has been invaluable.

CAN YOU FIND MY LOVE?
is dedicated to all children.

May each child be filled
with love and the fun for learning.

You have received this book
because someone loves you.

Look closely—you will find love hidden
in everyday things that you might
normally take for granted.

This is what it looks like.

When you find the love I have placed
for you, I hope that it warms your
heart and lets you know how
very special you are.

BABY animals
have their own names.

BABIES

PUP

A baby dog, armadillo, beaver or seal
is called a pup.

CAN YOU FIND MY LOVE?

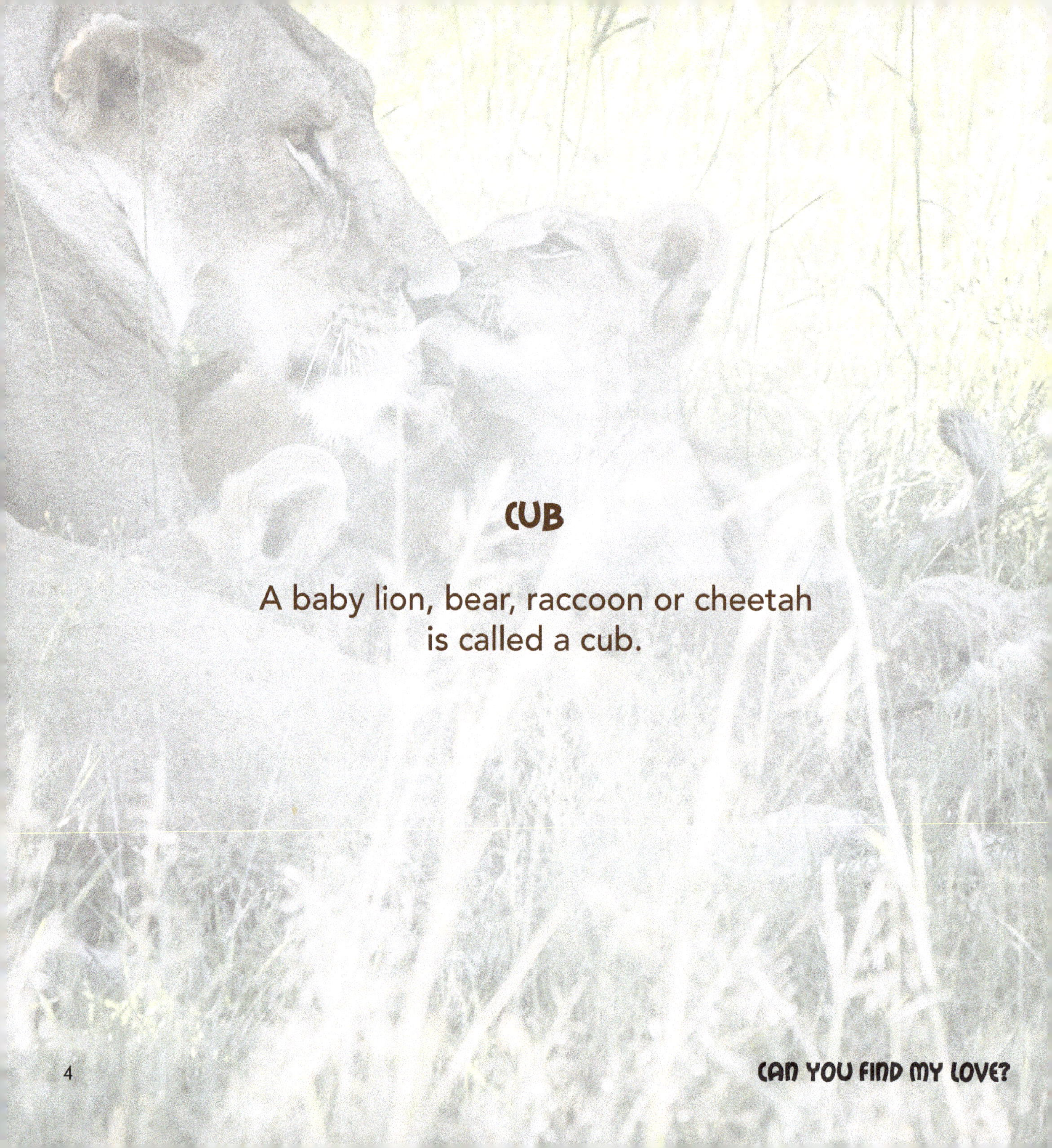

CUB

A baby lion, bear, raccoon or cheetah
is called a cub.

CALF

A baby buffalo, giraffe, elephant or cow
is called a calf.

CAN YOU FIND MY LOVE?

KITTEN

A baby cat or skunk
is called a kitten.

CAN YOU FIND MY LOVE?

CRIA

A baby alpaca or llama
is called a cria.

CAN YOU FIND MY LOVE?

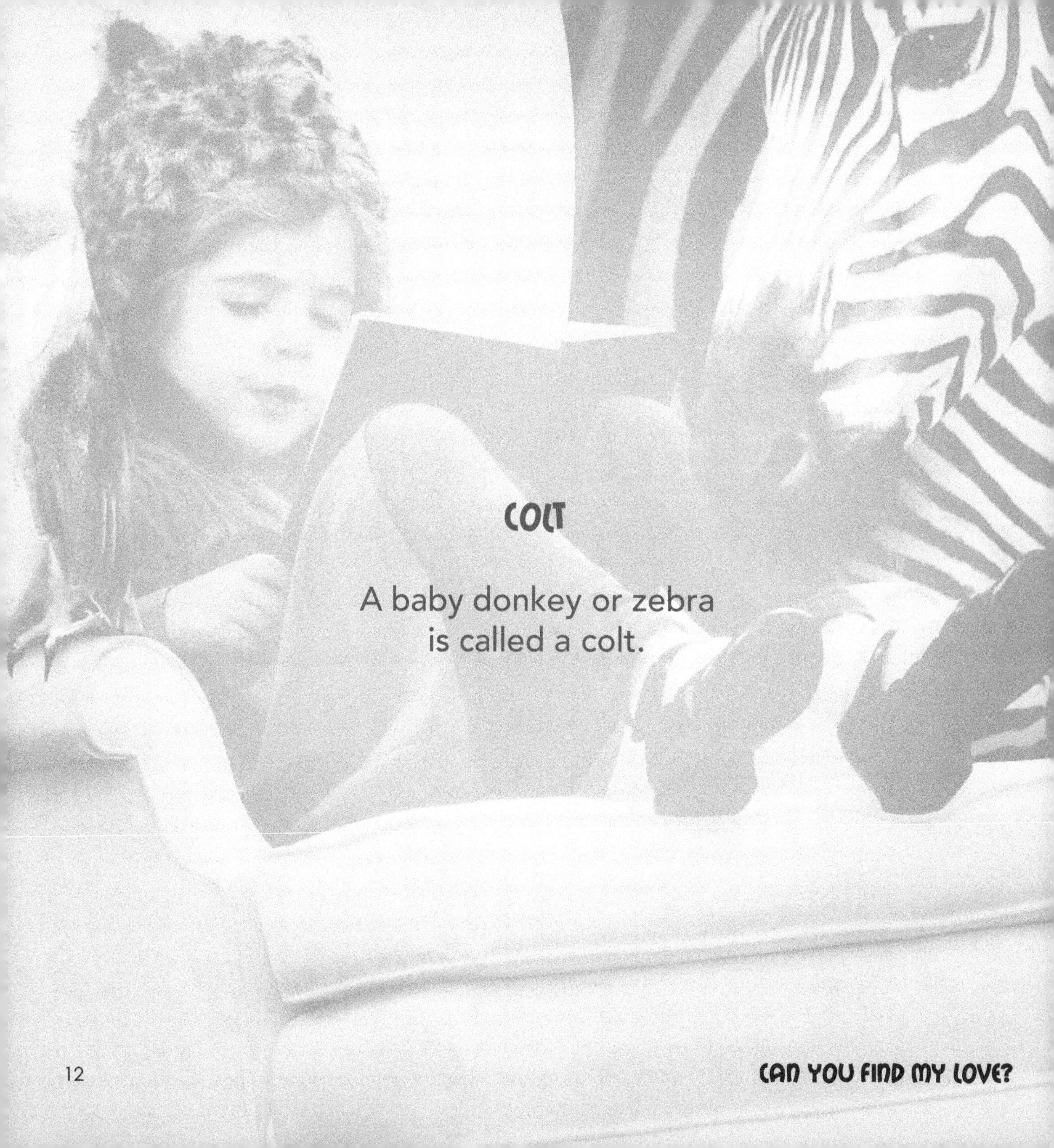

COLT

A baby donkey or zebra
is called a colt.

DUCKLING

A baby duck
is called a duckling.

CAN YOU FIND MY LOVE?

KID

A baby goat
is called a kid.

CAN YOU FIND MY LOVE?

INFANT

A baby gorilla, monkey or human
is called an infant.

CAN YOU FIND MY LOVE?

PIGLET

A baby pig or hedgehog
is called a piglet.

CAN YOU FIND MY LOVE?

FOAL & FILLY

A baby boy horse is called a foal
and a girl is called a filly.

CAN YOU FIND MY LOVE?

JOEY

A baby koala, wallaby, kangaroo or possum
is called a joey.

CAN YOU FIND MY LOVE?

ChICK

A baby penguin, ostrich or chicken
is called a chick.

CAN YOU FIND MY LOVE?

hATChLING

A baby alligator or dinosaur
is called a hatchling.

CAN YOU FIND MY LOVE?

FERRET

A baby ferret
is called a kit.

CAN YOU FIND MY LOVE?

GOSLING

A baby goose
is called a gosling.

CAN YOU FIND MY LOVE?

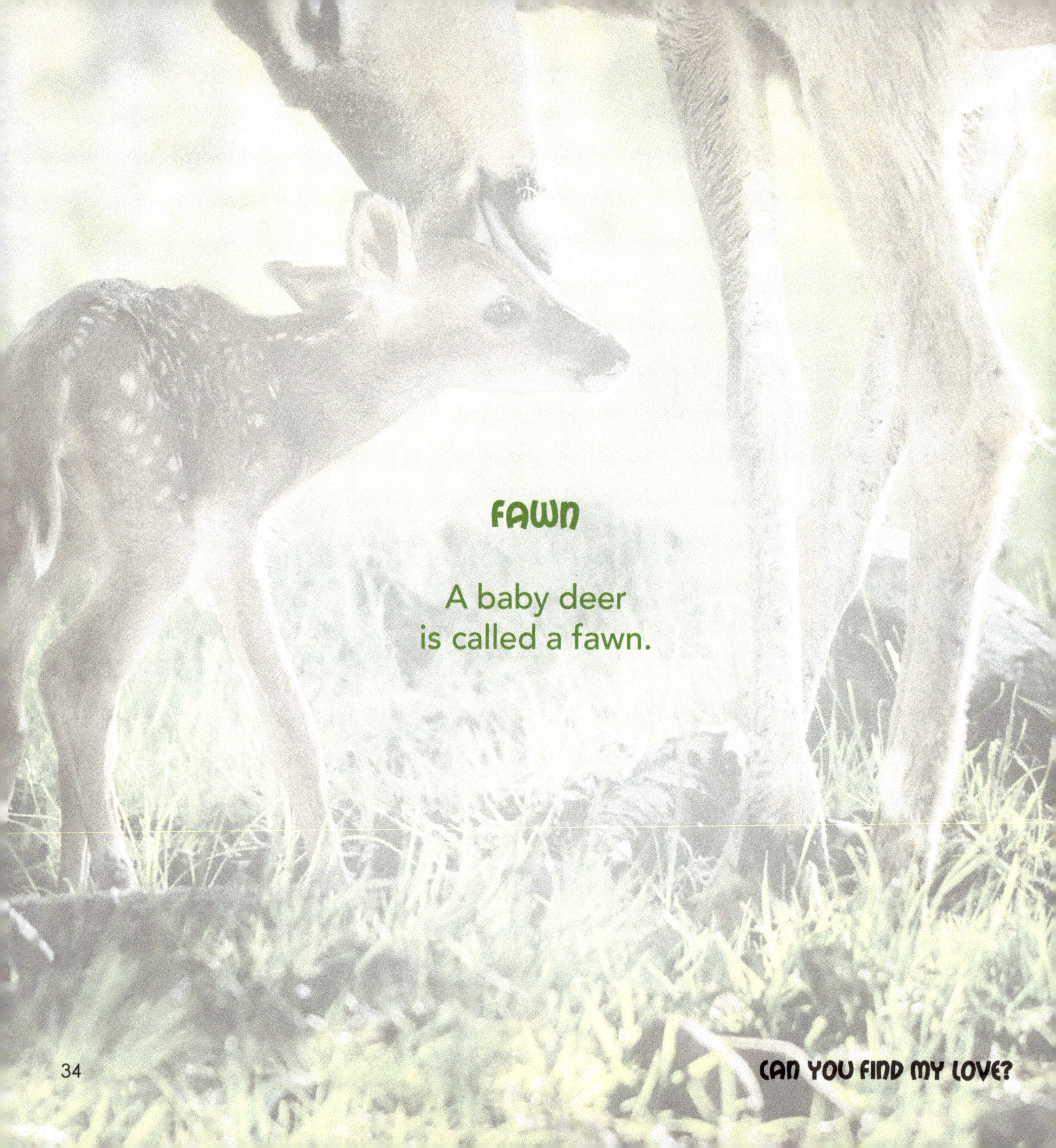

FAWN

A baby deer
is called a fawn.

CYGNET

A baby swan
is called a cygnet.

CAN YOU FIND MY LOVE?

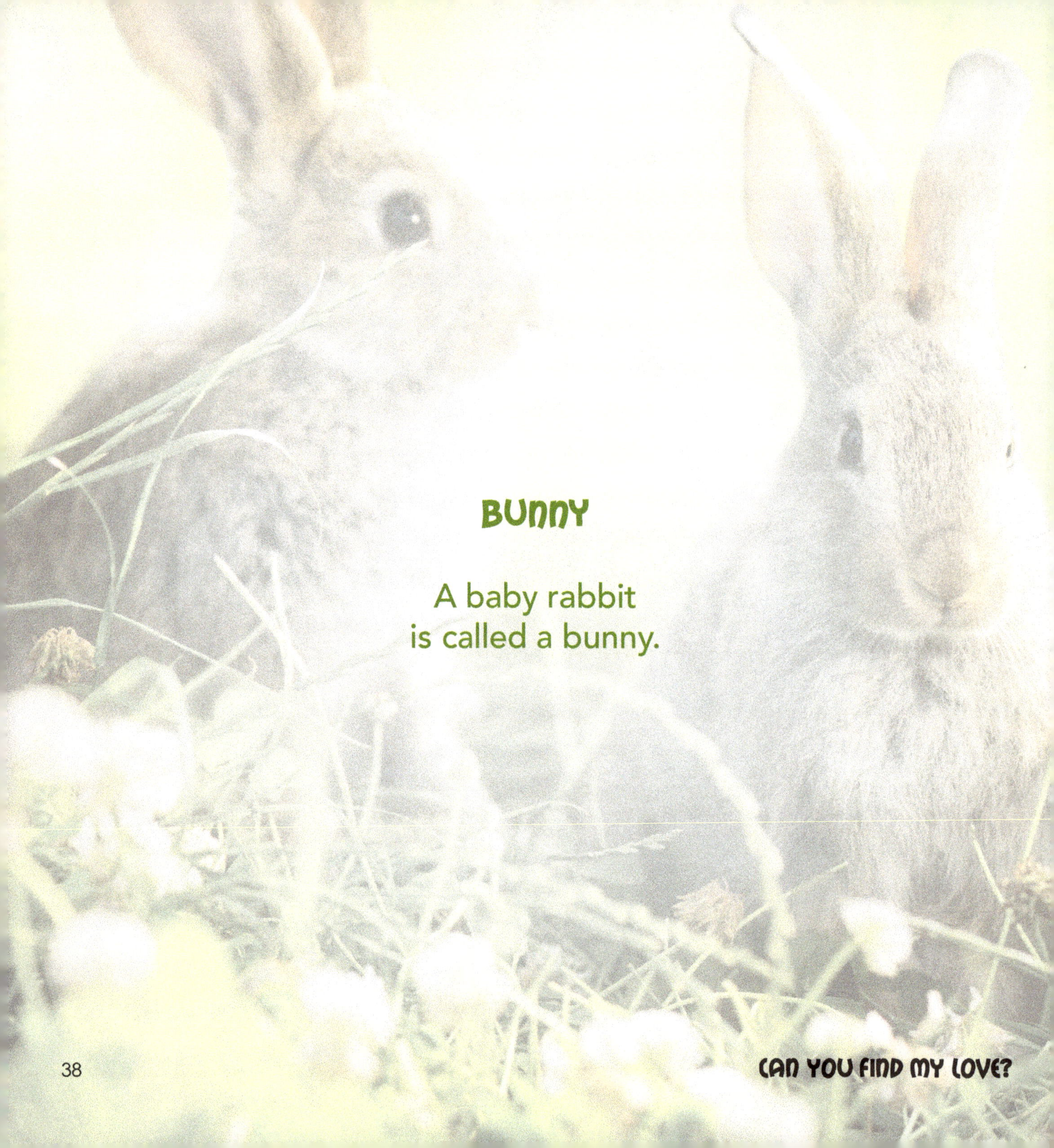

BUNNY

A baby rabbit
is called a bunny.

LAMB

A baby sheep
is called a lamb.

CAN YOU FIND MY LOVE?

TADPOLE

A baby frog
is called a tadpole.

CAN YOU FIND MY LOVE?

Did you look close enough
to find all my love?

Can you **DRAW** a few other **BABIES**?

Can you **DRAW** a few other **BABIES**?

Can you **DRAW** a few other **BABIES**?

From:

_____

NAME

About the Author

Jan Marquart is a psychotherapist and author. She has published 11 books for adults and has had articles, stories, poems and essays published in various newspapers, journals and magazines across the United States, Australia and Europe. She teaches writing for those over fifty and has taught a dozen writing workshops for Story Circle Network.

Jan has designed a 6-week writing course titled *Unveil the Wounded Self - Write to Heal* which focuses on healing PTSD and has also designed a 6-week writing course titled *The Provocation of Journal Writing* to encourage everyone to write their personal stories. She has written over 100 daily journals.

Jan can be contacted at JanMarquart.com, JanMarquartlcsw.wordpress.com and at her personal email address, jan@canyoufindmylove.com.

Her books can be purchased from all major online book retailers.

www.ingramcontent.com/pod-product-compliance
Lightning Source LLC
Chambersburg PA
CBHW040247100426
42811CB00011B/1185